I0830729

HOPE IN THE DARKNESS

HOPE IN THE DARKNESS

A GUIDE TO PREVENTING SUICIDE AND SAVING LIVES

HARRISON BLAIR

DEDICATION

To all those who have struggled in silence and felt the weight of despair, this book is for you. May you find hope in your darkest moments and know that you are not alone.

To the brave individuals who have shared their stories of recovery your courage inspires us all. And to the families, friends, and communities committed to supporting those in need, thank you for being the light in someone else's darkness.

Together, let us spread hope, foster understanding, and save lives.

Harrison Blair

TABLE OF CONTENTS

CHAPTER 1

〜〜〜〜〜〜〜〜〜〜〜〜〜〜〜〜〜〜〜〜〜〜〜〜〜〜〜〜〜〜〜〜〜〜〜〜〜

THE EFFECTS ON THE WORLD AND WHY THEY MATTER

I have been a clinical psychologist for ten years and have seen how suicide hurts families, neighborhoods, and society as a whole. Seeing someone commit suicide is not only a sorrow, it is also a public health emergency. Over 700,000 people die by suicide every year around the world, leaving a huge number of loved ones to deal with their pain. We are all affected by the mental toll, as well as the social and economic costs. This is why it's important.

Take Sarah, a 25-year-old woman who came to see me after her younger brother killed himself. She talked about how guilty and confused she felt all the time. Small changes in his behavior and a gradual pull away from things he used to enjoy were signs she had missed. Like many others, she didn't understand how important these changes were until it was too late. A lot of people have sad stories like hers, and they need to be told. Before it's too late, we need to be more aware of those who are at risk and take steps to help them.

Risk Factors and Signs of Trouble

Knowing the risk factors and warning signs is the first thing that can be done to stop people from committing suicide.

1

Suicide isn't caused by a single thing, but some situations make people more likely to do it. People who try to kill themselves often have mental health problems like sadness, anxiety, and drug abuse. Isolation, trauma, and big changes in life can make these problems worse.

In the case of Sarah's brother, his withdrawal and sudden lack of interest in activities were red flags that no one saw coming. He began giving away personal items, which is a common sign that someone might be thinking about committing suicide. This story isn't meant to scare you, it's meant to make you more aware of how small changes in behavior, even ones that don't seem important, can be big signs.

Let's learn to see what's going on below the surface to stop these kinds of tragedies. There are warning signs, and we can save lives if we pay attention and act. At this point in time, we can't afford to be quiet or do nothing.

Sarah's story should make you more careful, kind, and aggressive. To make a change, people need to know how common suicide is and what causes people to be at risk. We can change the story from one of loss and sorrow to one of hope and survival if we all work together.

CHAPTER 2

SUBTLE SIGNS AND BEHAVIORAL CUES

As a experience clinical psychologist, I've met a lot of people whose problems weren't clear at first. People who are thinking about suicide don't always make a loud plea for help. Often, it shows up in the quiet places of their behavior as small, almost unnoticeable changes. Being able to read these signs can mean the difference between life and death.

Let me tell you about James, a 40-year-old dad of two who came to see me because of what he called "work stress." He seemed calm, almost too calm for someone who said they were stressed out. He said he was tired, but said it was because he had been working long hours. At first glance, James looked like any other worker who was too busy. But there were little clues that something more important was going on. He stopped keeping plans with friends and family and avoided making eye contact when talking about how he felt.

When he talked about his kids, I noticed that he said he felt like a "burden" to them. That was a red flag a quiet sign that James was thinking about what he was worth and where he fit in their lives. These kinds of thoughts can be early signs of suicidal thoughts, especially if they happen along with pulling away from regular activities and feeling hopeless.

A very important point is made by James' story, big changes don't always mean that someone is in trouble. Some people's quiet pleas for help can be picked up in small changes in how they act, what they normally do, or the way they talk about their problems. Even though these signs may not seem important, they are. To spot them, you need to pay attention, understand, and be ready to ask tough questions.

Why early intervention is important

Early help is very important for stopping suicide. If we find someone at risk early on, we have a better chance of being able to help them and give them tools that can change their life. In James's case, we were able to help because we saw those early, minor signs. James learned how to deal with his strong feelings without giving up with the help of treatment and his family.

Early help is a tool that can save lives. The most important time to help someone is when they are feeling alone or stressed. Reaching out during this important time can stop suicidal ideas from getting worse.

Someone noticed James' change when they didn't hear what was being said out loud. His story shows how important it is to act not when the problem is obvious, but when the first signs of trouble start to show up. There is a skill to hearing the quiet plea that can save lives if we learn to pay close attention.

People you care about may change in small ways that you might not even notice. Pay attention to these changes. This is the time when someone can step in and stop a tragedy or restore hope. You could save someone's life if you learn to spot these subtle signs and move quickly.

CHAPTER 3

BREAKING THE STIGMA, CONVERSATIONS THAT SAVE LIVES

The shame that surrounds suicide is one of the hardest things I've seen in my ten years as a professional psychologist. Many people who are suffering stay quiet because they are afraid of being judged or misunderstood, which makes them feel even more alone. It is important to make sure that people feel comfortable talking about mental health and suicide, though, if we want to save lives.

I remember a young woman named Maria who was sent to me after she tried to kill herself but failed. It had been years since Maria had been depressed, but she never told anyone not her family or her friends. She didn't want to be called "weak" or "overdramatic." Because of the shame, she kept quiet, which pushed her closer to the edge. Maria finally let down her guard when she was in therapy and the therapists were kind to her instead of harsh.

Getting rid of the stigma is the first step in making these safe places. We need to get rid of the harmful stories that circle mental health problems and replace them with ones that help us understand. When people don't think they will be judged or ignored when they talk about their worst thoughts, they are more likely to get help before it's too late. Just changing the way we talk about mental health can make a big difference in how people feel about it.

How to Listen Well and Respond with Compassion

When someone tells you they are having suicidal ideas, the most important thing you can do is listen. Not just hear, but really listen. Giving someone your full attention, without interrupting or judging, and letting them talk about their pain in their own words is an important part of listening well.

I worked with a man named David who was having a hard time because he had lost his job and his sense of who he was. He hesitated and spoke in broken sentences during our first meeting because he wasn't sure if he could fully trust me with his thoughts. But I waited patiently, giving him space for silence when he needed it and asking him soft, open-ended questions. I made David feel heard, which was something he hadn't had in a long time. That was the first step in his recovery.

When you respond with understanding, you're not trying to "fix" the problem or give quick answers. People who care about someone in pain often tell them to "cheer up" or "think positively," but they don't mean it. They end up denying their feelings. The most helpful thing you can do is just be there, listen with care, and recognize how hard their situation is without downplaying it.

I didn't offer advice or clichés while David talked about his fears and lack of hope. He was having a tough time, so I told him, "It sounds like you're carrying a lot of pain right now, and that's really hard." David felt safe enough to keep talking because he knew he wasn't being judged or rushed through his thoughts.

Listening with empathy can change your life. When you make room for open conversation and listen, you give someone a chance to be seen, heard, and know that their pain is important. You don't have to know everything, but you don't need to. Someone can live because you are there, you are patient, and you care.

Maria and David are live proof that talking about suicide can bring back hope if you do it with someone who understands and cares. We can help people who need it most get better by getting rid of the shame and teaching them how to listen well. When someone comes to you with their problems, remember that being willing to have hard talks can save their life.

CHAPTER 4

PUTTING TOGETHER A SUPPORT SYSTEM, MAKING FRIENDS AND FAMILY STRONGER

Over the years as a professional psychologist, and one thing I have learned is that no one can get better from suicidal thoughts on their own. It's important to have a good support system. When someone is in trouble, family, friends, and experts can all help in different ways. They can save lives and keep tragedies from happening just by being there.

I will never forget the story of Alex, a college student who had been depressed for years without telling anyone. His family didn't know how much pain he was in. When Alex talked to a friend, who gently pushed him to get help, it became clear how bad his emotional problems really were. Alex was able to tell his parents about his problems because his friend was there for him and didn't judge him. They just listened and offered support.

People from family, friends, and work all have important roles to play, but they need to work together. When Alex's parents realized how bad things were for him, they came together to help him. They didn't give him answers right away, they just let him know they were there and loved him no matter what. They also knew what they weren't good at and got help from professionals. It took Alex some time to understand his feelings better and find better ways to deal with them after seeing a therapist.

Alex's story shows that friends and family are often the first people who help you out. They don't have to know everything, they just need to be there, caring, and ready to help their loved ones get skilled help. A strong support system connects someone who is having a hard time with the skilled help they need to get better.

How Communities Can Give People Hope

The community as a whole is very important in keeping people from committing suicide, not just close family and friends. People need a social structure to feel connected and respected, and communities provide that. When communities encourage open conversations about mental health, they send a clear message, it's okay to have problems and there is help out there.

I remember working in a small town with an extremely high suicide rate. This neighborhood was close, but no one brought up mental health problems. They didn't say anything because they were afraid of being seen as weak. But things changed when religious leaders, teachers, and neighborhood leaders got together to talk about mental health in an open way. They set up groups, got experts to talk, and told people they didn't have to feel bad about telling their stories.

Lisa, a young woman, did something brave at a community event one day, she spoke about how she overcame suicide thoughts. Her words spoke to a lot of people, especially teens who had been suffering in silence. More and more people started to ask for help after seeing how brave she was. They decided to break the silence and help each other, which made this community an example of hope and healing.

I learned from this that when communities make it normal to talk about mental health, they make a safe and accepting space for everyone. People feel safe enough to ask for help there without worrying about being judged.

Support groups are bigger than one person. They're an important part of families, friendships, and neighborhoods. Building stronger ties between people gives us hope that can catch people who feel like they are falling.

Along with Alex's family and Lisa's neighborhood, you can be a part of that net. Your part is important, whether it's to have a compassionate conversation, listen, or just be there. We can make support services that help people when they need it most stronger if we all work together. Communities that support mental health understanding and help people connect with each other save lives.

CHAPTER 5

TREATMENTS AND THERAPIES DONE BY PROFESSIONALS

As a clinical psychologist, I've seen how professional methods and treatments can change lives that seemed hopeless at first. Having access to the right tools can mean the difference between hope and despair for people who are having suicidal thoughts. The first step to getting better is to understand what professional help means.

Ethan, a 32-year-old software worker who is one of my patients, came to see me after months of being very depressed. He was at his wits' end and admitted that he had been thinking about killing himself for weeks. Ethan wasn't sure that therapy could help when we first started going together. Over time, though, he realized that professional help wasn't meant to fix him, it was meant to help him understand his feelings, find ways to deal with them, and rebuild his sense of self-worth.

There are many kinds of treatments, and each person reacts to them in their own way. Cognitive Behavioral Therapy (CBT) is one of the most common ways to help people who are having suicidal feelings. It helps people recognize and change the negative thought patterns that keep them feeling lost. Another good method is Dialectical Behavior Therapy (DBT), which focuses on controlling emotions and learning how to deal with problems. This can be especially helpful for people who are going through a crisis.

When recommended by a psychiatrist and closely watched by them, medication can also help stabilize mood and ease the symptoms of depression and anxiety that make suicidal thoughts more likely. For Ethan, CBT and medicine worked together to help him take back control of his life. He learned to keep his feelings and thoughts in check so they didn't get too sad.

It's not a sign of weakness to get help from a professional. It's a step toward healing and getting back in charge. Professionals such as therapists, counselors, and psychiatrists can help you deal with the complicated feelings that come with having suicidal ideas. Their knowledge can save people who are feeling hopeless because of their problems.

Crisis lines, support groups, and helplines

In addition to individual therapy, people who are in trouble can also use other important services. When someone feels like they have nowhere else to turn, helplines, support groups, and crisis interventions can be reached right away and offer warmth and support.

I used to work with a young woman named Priya who had suicidal ideas but was afraid to tell anyone who knew her. It was too much for her to handle, and she wasn't ready to talk to a doctor. It got so bad in her mind one night that she called a suicide prevention service. Because the talk was private, she could say what was really bothering her without worrying about what other people would think. It saved her life because it was the first thing she did to get help.

Helplines, such as the National Suicide Prevention Lifeline or the Crisis Text Line, are run by trained professionals and volunteers who can help you right away. They're there for people 24/7 when they need to talk, and they're a lifesaver in times of trouble. These services can also help people find other tools, like therapy or inpatient care if that's what they need.

Support groups are also very helpful because they give people a safe place to talk to others who are going through the same problems. Sharing your story with a group can help you feel less alone and more connected to others. Many people feel a lot better when they know they're not the only ones having these feelings and thoughts.

Crisis intervention teams, which are often part of hospitals or community health groups, help people who are seriously considering suicide right away. These steps, like emergency mental care or mobile crisis units that can go to people's homes, help quickly and save lives when time is of the essence.

After calling the helpline, Priya did go to therapy, but that first talk was very important. It made her brave enough to do what she needed to do. Helplines, support groups, and crisis assistance aren't just useful tools, they're also ways to connect with others right away, when it's most needed.

No one should have suicidal ideas by themselves. Professional help, neighborhood support, and crisis resources are all important parts of a complete plan to stop people from committing suicide. Remember that help is always available if you or someone you know is having a hard time. You don't have to go through this process by yourself. There is hope, and the first step is to reach out.

CHAPTER 6

USEFUL TIPS FOR PEOPLE WHO ARE IN CRISIS

I've seen directly how self-care and coping skills can help people deal with emotional pain. These tools are important for everyone who wants to keep their mental health in good shape, not just people who are in a crisis. When you feel like your feelings of hopelessness are about to take over, having useful skills on hand can save you.

Mia, one of my clients, reached out to me when things were really bad in her life. She felt like she was always in a crisis because she was depressed and anxious. During our meetings, we started to talk about different ways for her to take care of herself that would work for her. Mindfulness practice was one method that spoke to her. Mia learned to pay attention to her breath and her thoughts without judging them. This helped her feel less connected to her strong feelings.

Writing in a book is another useful tool. I told Mia to write down how she felt and what she was thinking when she didn't want to say them out loud. Writing gave her a safe place to work through her feelings, figure out what set them off, and think about her progress. She discovered that writing in a journal not only helped her understand things better, but it also let go of the emotional weight she was holding.

Being active is also a key part of dealing with mental pain. Even short walks in nature every day helped Mia connect with her surroundings and find peace. Endorphins are chemicals that are released when you exercise. They can make you feel better and less anxious. A feeling of well-being can come from doing small things like yoga or stretching.

Self-care is all about finding what works best for you. These techniques can be changed to fit each person's tastes, whether that's spending time in nature, being creative, or practicing gratitude. The goal is to give each person a personalized set of tools for dealing with mental pain that they can use when they need help.

Helping Family and Friends Become Stronger

Self-care is important for people who are going through a disaster, but it's also important to help loved ones become more resilient. When someone we care about is having a hard time, we can play a big part in helping them get through it and build a better mental health foundation.

I worked with a dad named Robert whose daughter Lily, who was in high school, had just been through a very hard time. Robert didn't know what to do to help her and felt powerless. We talked about how he could be a caring presence in Lily's life while also encouraging her to develop her own self-care habits.

One important step was encouraging open conversation. Robert learned how to give Lily a place where she could talk about her feelings without worrying about being judged. He made her feel valuable and understood by asking her open-ended questions and really listening to what she had to say. This made their relationship stronger and also made Lily more willing to talk about her problems.

I also showed Robert how to take care of himself by doing the same things. He started talking about how he dealt with stress by doing things like taking breaks to relax, doing hobbies, and making family time a priority. He sent the word that it's okay to ask for help and put your own health first by showing how important it is to do so.

Support groups can also help family and friends. Meeting people who have been through the same problems can help you feel like you're part of a group and help you understand each other better. Robert pushed Lily to join a youth support group, which helped her become stronger by letting her share her own experiences and learn from them.

Giving someone power is a big part of helping them through a problem. You can help your loved ones build the resilience they need to deal with life's challenges by encouraging them to look into ways to take care of themselves, promoting open conversation, and acting in a healthy way yourself.

Self-care and ways to deal with stress are not just ways to stay alive, they are also ways to heal and grow. We build a culture of resilience that can handle life's stresses when we follow these habits and encourage the people we care about to do the same. It's impossible to say enough about how important self-care is on the path to mental health. It is a powerful way to deal with inner pain.

CHAPTER 7

~~~~~~

REAL LIFE ACCOUNTS OF PEOPLE WHO OVERCAME SUICIDAL THOUGHTS

Being a professional psychologist for many years has given me the chance to see amazing changes happen. Some people have gone through the darkness of suicidal thoughts and come out into the light. Their stories are strong reminders that recovery is possible and can lead to a complete new start.

Lisa's story is one of these kinds. She is a lively artist who used to have crippling sadness. Lisa was so sad and hopeless after her mother died that she thought about committing suicide. She often felt alone because she thought no one could understand how much pain she was in. She didn't start to see things differently until she joined a neighborhood support group. Hearing other people talk about their problems helped her see that she wasn't the only one.

Lisa found the strength to express her feelings artistically with the help of the group and her ongoing therapy. Art helped her get better by letting her turn her sadness into something beautiful. Lisa now uses her story to motivate others and holds classes to help people who are hurting find their own creative ways to deal with their feelings. Her story shows that even in the worst situations, hope and healing can come out of
~~~~~~

them.

Another powerful story is that of James, a veteran who had PTSD and suicidal ideas after he got home from the military. He was angry and helpless for years and couldn't talk about his problems with the people around him. He didn't find a group of people who understood and shared his feelings until he joined a program to help soldiers.

James learned to face his feelings instead of ignoring them through therapy and help from his friends. He started to be more mindful and do physical things like hiking, which helped him get back in touch with himself and nature. Today, James works to raise awareness about mental health issues among soldiers and encourages others to do the same. He says that asking for help is a sign of strength, not weakness.

These stories show that getting better is not a straight line. The journey of each person is different and has its own ups and downs, but they all have one thing in common, hope.

How it's possible to have hope and heal

Hope is a strong force that can bring about change. It can make you want to get help, connect with others, and work toward a better life. As a therapist, I've seen that hope often grows in the strangest places, like when people help each other, when people express themselves creatively, or when people realize that healing is a process, not a goal.

For many, getting better starts with taking one step, admitting they are in pain and asking for help. It's important to understand that recovery doesn't mean not having any problems. Instead, it means getting the tools and strength to deal with problems as they come up. This is where support groups, therapy, and taking care of yourself come in handy.

Lisa and James showed that telling their story can be very powerful, for both the person telling it and the people listening to it. Survivors break down the stigma around mental health problems when they talk freely about their experiences. Their stories give other people hope and encourage them to get help, showing that healing is possible.

On the path to healing, there are many chances to start over. People who have had suicidal thoughts often come out of it with a better understanding of who they are, a renewed sense of purpose, and a promise to help others through their problems. They become lights of hope that show us all that we can get better even when things look bad.

Finally, let the stories of Lisa and James move you. There is always a way to get better, no matter how bad things look. Even when things are very hard, hope can grow, and we can find our way back to the light through connection, strength, and self-discovery. Whether you are having a hard time or are helping someone who is, know that recovery is not just possible, many people have been through it before you.

CHAPTER 8

<hr>

ACTION FOR PREVENTION STRATEGIES

During my time as a clinical psychologist, I saw firsthand how important it is for people, groups, and organizations to work together to stop suicide. Each group is very important, and if we all work together, we can build a strong support system that improves mental health and saves lives.

To begin, each of us can learn more about mental health problems and the signs of suicidal thoughts. Being aware is very helpful; the more we know, the better we can help people who need it. Little things, like checking in on family and friends, can make a big difference. I remember a client named Sarah who changed her relationships by getting to know the people in her group. Her simple question, "Are you okay?" led to deeper conversations and made people who were having a hard time feel seen and cared for.

Communities are also very important when it comes to preventing suicide. Health services, schools, and community groups in your area can work together to make mental health awareness programs, workshops, and support groups that encourage open conversations. A group of schools, churches, and companies in the area where I worked came together to start "Mental Health Awareness Month." They put together events, invited speakers, and gave people tools that taught people and pushed them to ask for help when they needed it. Because of this, a lot more people reached out for help, showing that community action can really help lower stigma and bring people together.

Active methods need to be used by all organizations, but especially those in health care and education. This can include teaching staff how to spot signs of worry and know how to help. It was my job to give advice to a high school where teachers were taught how to give mental health first aid. The initiative gave teachers the tools they needed to spot kids who were at risk and help them get help right away, which created a culture of support in the school.

Making a Plan Ahead of Time to Save Lives

For a prevention plan to work, it's important to make a proactive one that includes teaching, outreach, and support. A plan like this could look like this:

- *Education and Training:* Teach people and experts how to spot signs of distress, how to communicate clearly, and how to help someone find the right resources. It's possible to do this through events in the neighborhood, workshops, or online classes.

- *Support Systems:* Set up support systems that are easy for people to get to, like helplines, counseling services, and peer support groups. Make sure that these tools are widely known and easy for people who need them to find.

- *Community Engagement:* Hold events in your community that focus on wellness, resilience, and connection to encourage people to talk openly about their mental health. Get groups in your area to work together on projects that raise understanding about mental health.

- *Crisis Intervention:* Make clear crisis intervention procedures that tell people what to do if they or someone they know is in immediate danger. This can include training for people who work in mental health and emergency services.

- *Follow-Up and Support:* Set up programs to help people who have asked for help before. Regular check-ins can help them feel supported and linked, which lowers the risk of them feeling alone.

- *Comments Mechanism:* Make a way for people in the community to give comments on mental health programs and resources. This can help groups change their plans so they can better meet the needs of the people they help.

This plan to be responsible isn't just a theory, it's a call to action. For suicide to not happen, we all need to do our part. As a friend, family member, teacher, or leader in the community, what you do can turn things around and save lives.

Let us work together as people, as communities, and as organizations to create a space where mental health is valued, where getting help is encouraged, and where hope grows. We can make progress toward a world with fewer suicide deaths by working together and using these strategies. We can make the world a better place by working together. Everyone will feel respected, connected, and able to ask for help when they need it.

CONCLUSION

A BRIGHT FUTURE

As we come to the end of "Hope in the Darkness," it's important to think about the ongoing work to stop suicide and the important part we all play in it. It is a strong reminder that we can make changes in our own lives and in the lives of those around us through the stories, strategies, and ideas in these chapters.

Stopping suicide isn't just a one-time thing, it's an ongoing effort to create a community of understanding, compassion, and help. As a group, we can save lives with every talk we start, every connection we keep alive, and every resource we share. The goal is clear, we need to keep learning about mental health, stop the stigma that surrounds it, and speak up for people who may feel like they have no voice.

As humans, we can give people in trouble a sense of hope. If we can spot the signs of mental distress in our loved ones and offer a caring hand, we can help them get the help they need. Healing is not just possible, it's a journey of change that is full of growth and possibility. Stories of recovery and renewal remind us of this.

There is also a very important part for communities. When people work together to make mental health conversations feel safe, they build support networks that give people the confidence to ask for help. Mental health programs not only teach, but also help people feel like they belong and are connected, which reminds us that we are not alone in our difficulties.

Also, groups working in health care, education, or community services need to keep pushing for mental health tools and proactive strategies. They can make the workplace more supportive by putting in place training, support systems, and outreach programs. This will make asking for help normal and encouraged.

Suicide prevention is an ongoing process. The problems that need to be solved may seem impossible, but there is a huge chance for things to get better. We can build a culture that values mental health as an important part of overall well-being by giving hope and help to those who need it.

Let's take on this task with compassion and speed, knowing that what we do together can lead to a bright future. A world where everyone feels like they are important, understood, and have the power to ask for help. As we move forward, let us stay alert, dedicated, and motivated by the strength of those who have overcome hardships. We can make a world full of hope and save lives if we all work together.

www.ingramcontent.com/pod-product-compliance
Lightning Source LLC
Chambersburg PA
CBHW061325250726
48657CB00003B/1042